It's a Hummingbird's Life

Irene Kelly

Holiday House / New York

MANHASSET PUBLIC LIBRARY

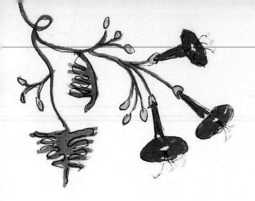

For my mother, Ann Kelly

Copyright © 2003 by Irene Kelly
All Rights Reserved
Printed in the United States of America
www.holidayhouse.com
First Edition

Library of Congress Cataloging-in-Publication Data
Kelly, Irene.
It's a hummingbird's life/Irene Kelly.—1st ed.
p. cm.
ISBN 0-8234-1658-5 (hardcover)
1. Hummingbirds—Juvenile literature. [1. Hummingbirds.] I. Title.
QL696.A558 K45 2002
598.7'64—dc21   00-053544

male

What is a hummingbird's life?

Very, very busy! All year round.

female

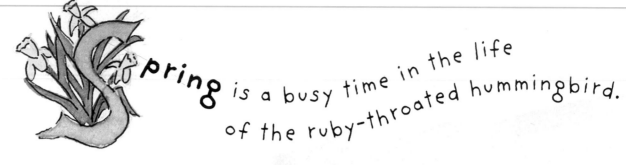

Spring is a busy time in the life of the ruby-throated hummingbird.

Nest materials can be almost anything.

milkweed seeds

twigs

feathers

spider silk

It begins with the gigantic job of building a tiny, tiny nest.

The nest is only as big as half a Ping-Pong ball!

This nest has poodle fur in it.

The female builds it by stitching the walls together with spider silk, gluing them with saliva, and stamping a soft cottony down into the lining with her feet. Then she adds lichen and moss to the outside as camouflage.

A single penny fits snugly in the nest.

After the nest is ready (or nearly so), the female sets off in search of a mate. When she finds one, he performs a dazzling aerial display.

diving and swooping

Males always face the sun during performances.
They want to show off their glittery, shimmering feathers in the best light.
(There's not much mating on cloudy days.)

Mating lasts from 3 to 5 seconds, then the birds go their separate ways.

The male resumes his busy day's work while the female zips back to her nest.

Hummingbirds lay 2 very tiny eggs. Each weighs less than one-half a gram. You could mail 60 eggs with one postage stamp!

actual size

JB Nelson

Derek + Lucy
Main St.
Maplewood. NJ
0 7 0 4 0

The expectant mother settles in, like a perfect lid on a perfect pot.

The female sits on the eggs to keep them warm until they hatch 15 to 20 days later.

The newborns look like raisins with a thin cover of downy feathers along their backs.

At first, the hatchlings are fed every 3 minutes. The mother plunges her bill down their throats, depositing food.

The mother eats 2000 insects every day.

Twelve days after they are born, the babies are covered with feathers.

day 12

Newborns keep the nest neat by sitting on the edge and letting their droppings fall to the ground.

day 14

Another week later, they are flapping their wings.

Soon the chicks begin to practice flying by hanging onto the rim of the nest and "humming" their wings. By day 30, they are ready to fly.

"humming"

They're off!

At this point, the mother's job is done. She may check on her young a few more times, but the chicks are ready to begin their solitary life—while the mother raises a new brood.

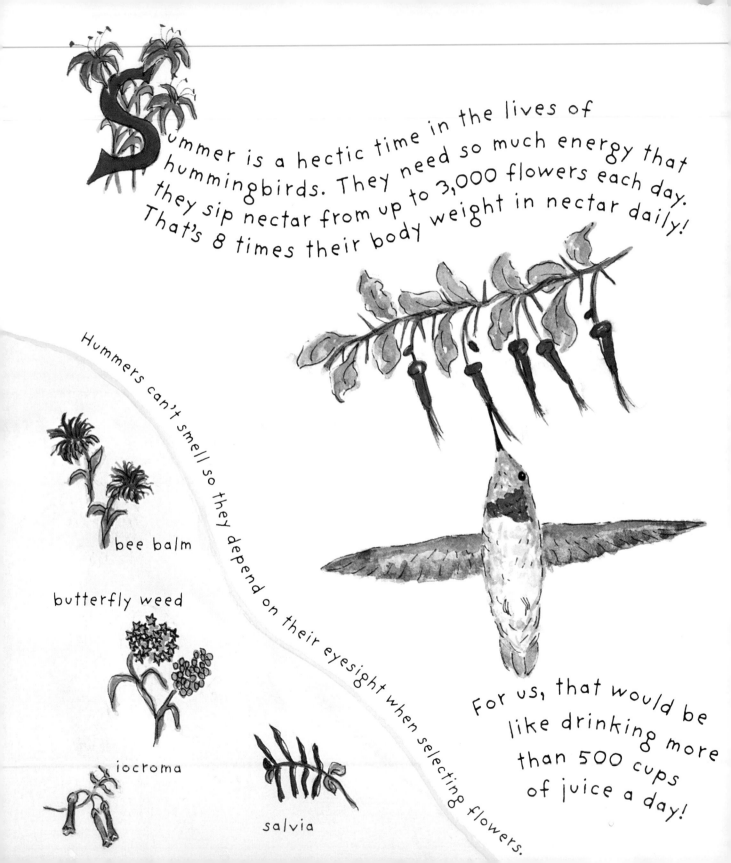

Summer is a hectic time in the lives of hummingbirds. They need so much energy that they sip nectar from up to 3,000 flowers each day. That's 8 times their body weight in nectar daily!

Hummers can't smell so they depend on their eyesight when selecting flowers.

bee balm

butterfly weed

iocroma

salvia

For us, that would be like drinking more than 500 cups of juice a day!

Hummers work even as they feed.
They rarely perch. Instead,
they hover in midair as they eat.
They especially love red, tube-shaped blossoms.

trumpet creeper

They snatch aphids while they're flying and gobble up gnats from spiderwebs. Sometimes they even eat the spider!

Hummingbirds also work at staying clean. They bathe in tiny puddles on leaves or soak in a rain shower or lawn sprinkler.

Hummers love to bathe on leaves.

After splashing about, hummers groom
and preen their feathers, feet, and beaks.

They also love to sunbathe. They face the sun,
fluff out their feathers, and bask in the warmth.
It's an unusually peaceful time for this energetic bird.

Once a hummingbird finds an area with lots of food, it claims the territory. No visitors are allowed. If a creature does intrude, the hummingbird will:

puff out its chest, spread its tail, and toss its head about.

That's usually enough to frighten off the intruder. If that doesn't work, it will chase and attack the trespasser no matter who it is:

a cat, a crow, or maybe even you and me!

Sometimes hummingbirds fight with each other like tiny swordsmen!

Although they aren't friendly, hummers have only a few enemies. Some frogs and large fish have been known to leap up, catch a hummingbird, and pull it underwater.

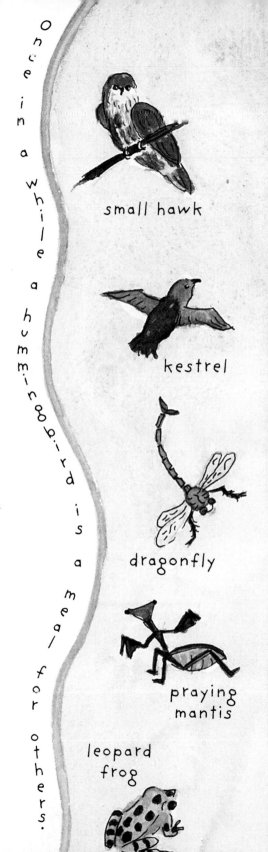

Once in a while a hummingbird is a meal for others.

small hawk

kestrel

dragonfly

praying mantis

leopard frog

Hummingbirds can rotate their wings
in a full circle, just like a helicopter's blades.
That's why they can hover and fly backward,
and even fly upside down!

They can also lift themselves straight into the air.

Fall may be the busiest time for the very busy hummingbird. This is when the hummers migrate south for the winter.

North America

Florida

Mexico

Central America

As soon as it gets nippy, most U.S. hummers take off for Mexico or South and Central America, where they will spend the winter.

Ruby-throated hummingbirds begin by flying solo for several days until they reach Florida. There they fatten up and wait for good weather to begin the last leg of their journey.

Atlantic Ocean

South America

Florida has new flowers for hummingbirds to try.

cypress vine

lantana

butterfly bush

lobelia

Hummingbirds are experts at predicting the weather. They leave Florida only when there is a steady northwesterly wind, clear skies, and no hint of a storm coming.

The tiny birds' wings beat very fast:

3,000 times per minute or approximately 4,500,000 times by the time the hummers reach Mexico.

They set off across the Gulf of Mexico, skimming low over the waves. Their trip will take about 25 hours at the rate of 25 miles per hour.

For a long time, no one believed that such a small bird could survive this long and difficult journey without help. Some people thought the hummingbird hitched a ride on the back of a Canada goose! A lovely idea but not true.

Besides the occasional fishing boat, the only place for a hummingbird to rest during this flight is on a hot air balloon!

Sometimes balloonists hang feeders from their basket
to give the voyager a much-appreciated snack.
The tiny birds keep going, even after the sun sets.

Winter is also an active time in the lives of hummingbirds, but they begin slowly. The first thing they do after their exhausting journey across the Gulf is rest.

Some hummingbirds may enter "torpor" when going to sleep. Hummingbirds choose to become torpid when they are extremely hungry, tired, or cold. During torpor, their body temperature drops and their heart rate slows, and they are able to conserve energy till morning.

It can take a full hour to wake up from this deeply sleepy state.

stretching

Hummingbirds in torpor are so still and silent, they can appear to be dead. In the past, lots of people believed hummingbirds had magical powers that allowed them to die, then come back to life.

A few things hummingbirds do not do in winter:

nest

mate

lay eggs

Once the birds are rested, they must eat. But after just a couple days of resting and feeding, hummingbirds take off in search of winter homes.

coral bean

Mexican sage

Mexican cigar

shrimp plant

anise sage

Mexico offers tropical treats.

Some will journey as far south as Belize or Guatemala, while others will find a nearby patch of woodland and settle in.

Some hummers choose to live at the edge of a farm or on the grounds of a plantation. A number of especially adventurous hummingbirds will travel deep into the jungle! They all must find a territory with plenty of food not yet claimed by another bird.

The hummingbird will spend an action-packed 5 months defending its territory, zipping from flower to flower, bathing, preening, and sunbathing before heading back to the United States for another busy year.

Long-Tailed Hermit
Mexico, Central and South America

Sparkling-Tailed
Mexico, Central America

White-Bellied Emerald
Mexico, Central America

This book is about the ruby-throated hummingbird, but there are 343 different types of hummingbirds. Fifteen kinds live in the western United States,

Striped-Tailed
Mexico, Central America

Racket-Tailed
Ecuador, Venezuela,
Bolivia

Broad-Tailed
North America,
Mexico, Guatemala

and just the ruby-throated hummingbird
lives east of the Mississippi River. All the
other species live in South and Central America.

Want to see hummingbirds up close?
Plant their favorite flowers in a container or
window box, or in your garden, and they will
visit your home!

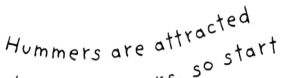

lantana

salvia

petunia

Hummers are attracted
to red flowers, so start
with a few of those: salvia, cypress vine, parrots beak,
or fuchsia. Once they have discovered your red flowers,
they will happily dine from blossoms of any color.

cypress vine

honeysuckle

impatiens

parrots beak

J
598.764
K

Kelly, Irene.
It's a
hummingbird's
life

16.95

WITHDRAWN

SEP 1 6 2003

Manhasset Public Library
Manhasset, NY 11030
Telephone: 627-2300